MEL BAY PRESENTS

THE ART OF TWO-LINE IMPROVISATION

by Jimmy Wyble

edited and recorded by David Oakes

CD CONTENTS

1 Etude 7 [1:35]	9 Etude 15 [:58]	16 Etude 22 [1:48]
2 Etude 8 [1:42]	10 Etude 16 [:56]	17 Etude 23 [1:19]
3 Etude 9 [3:21]	11 Etude 17 [2:01]	18 Etude 24 [:53]
4 Etude 10 [2:39]	12 Etude 18 [:54]	19 Etude 25 [3:34]
5 Etude 11 [1:07]	13 Etude 19 [:58]	20 Improvisation Part One [2:23]
6 Etude 12 [1:03]	14 Etude 20 [:54]	21 Improvisation Part Two [1:16]
7 Etude 13 [3:47]	15 Etude 21 [1:23]	22 Improvisation 24 Part Two [:43]
8 Etude 14 [1:00]		

Visit us on the Web at www.melbay.com — E-mail us at email@melbay.com

What guitarists said about the first edition:

"Fresh new literature for guitarists" — Joe Pass

"Jimmy Wyble is one of the greatest guitar talents" — Laurindo Almedia   Guitar Player - June 1977

"The result of a true master displaying melodic, harmonic, and rhythmic artistry . . . a must in every guitar players library." — Tony Rizzi

"Some of the most inventive music ever written for guitar . . . .Jimmy Wyble is one of my favorite players." — Mundell Lowe

What guitarists are saying about Jimmy Wyble and this new edition:

Jimmy has a rare ability to create beautiful and complete musical statements through the use of two line counterpoint. These works have the depth and economy of Picasso's line drawings and the musical magnitude of Bach's inventions. Jimmy is a complete master of the art of improvisation.
— Larry Koonse
Performer
California Institute of the Arts Faculty

When I first heard these etudes I recognized instantly that this was another league of guitar playing and guitar composition. After the initial shock wore off, I realized that I could no longer ignore counterpoint in my playing.
These beautiful etudes are among the most important works written for the guitar in the 20th century and is one of the reasons the name of Jimmy Wyble is held in reverence by so many guitarists. These etudes should be an essential part of every guitarists library.
David Oakes masterful performance and meticulous transcriptions have made this work possible in its present form. For this, the guitar world is enriched.
— Sid Jacobs

After reading through Jimmy's etudes and standard tune arrangements, I began to incorporate some of his concepts into my playing. I'm very grateful to this master musician for his great contribution to the guitar.
Thanks Jimmy,
— Joe Diorio

It doesn't get any better than Jimmy Wyble. As a guitarist and a composer he is a very intuitive as well as a creative musician. "A natural!"
— Ron Escheté

Jimmy Wyble's music is unique, in the truest sense of the word. It is original in musical content and also in the guitar techniques needed to play it. Any player who can put forth the effort to learn some of these etudes will no doubt improve as a musician as well as a guitarist. The music is simply beautiful.
David Oakes has helped revive this important music and has presented it flawlessly. The recording and the engraving with absolute attention to detail, make exploring this music a pleasure! Great job and many thanks David!
To Jimmy.....Thanks! Your influence changed the way I play guitar and opened me up to a whole new concept on the guitar. God bless, and thanks for the lessons.
— Bruce Buckingham
Fingerstylist everywhere will delight in and benefit from this incredible selection of Jimmy Wyble's etudes, meticulously edited by David Oakes.
— Chas Grasamke

Jimmy Wyble has created some beautiful etudes that combine the best of the jazz and classical worlds. He has made an important contribution to the guitar repertoire and David Oakes has done a wonderful job cleaning up, editing and recording Jimmy's material.
— John Stowell

When Jimmy Wyble played some of these pieces in public during the mid '70's, he was the talk of the town amongst many of the finer guitar players. The music is brilliant and exciting, yet often also intellectually stimulating. Some pieces are bluesy, others intriguingly dissonant, still others tender and beautiful, even a dash of Flamenco here and there - overall, quite an array of rich colors. Certain moments may likely dazzle you with their rhythmic ingenuity, other with a wild turn of harmony or melody, all bathed quite often in a feast of counterpoint.

When people ask me to describe this music, one way I'm fond of is:

George Van Eps meets Bartok and they visit T. Monk to discuss the music of J.S. Bach and a certain Mr. Gershwin. . . . .
— Ted Greene

"Jimmy exercises and etudes combine innovative counterpoint, refreshing rhythmic and harmonic ideas into fresh and exciting literature. His musical gifts match his loving and generous spirit perfectly. I respect him enormmously both as a musician and a humanitarian."
— Ron Berman

Acknowledgments

The Art of Two Line Improvisation is an adventure in new fingering concepts for the Classical and Jazz guitarist. I am moved by the beautiful and powerful playing of David Oakes and appreciate his interest in this music.

I dedicate the music to the Studio Jazz and Classical guitar departments of the University of Southern California where I had the opportunity to work with Duke Miller, James Smith and many of the distinguished teachers.

I deeply appreciate the support of Sid Jacobs and Ron Berman in getting the *Art of Two Line Improvisation* and *Classical/Country* into completion. I look to Ron Berman, Sid Jacobs, David Oakes and Larry Koonse's generation of guitarist for inspiration. They are very accomplished teachers and performers.

Much Love to All,

Jimmy Wyble

My participation in this book as an editor as well as making the recording was a true labor of love. Thank you Jimmy for letting me participate in this important project. I would like to thank Bruce Buckingham, Sid Jacobs and Ron Benson. These three incredible guitarist/musicians have spent many hours over the years helping me to better understand Jimmy Wyble's music. Finally I would like to recognize Vaso Dimitriou. As a recording engineer and as a music transcriber extraordinaire, her input into this project was invaluable.

David Oakes

Foreword for the new edition

Every now and then a guitarist comes on the jazz scene with a completely unique playing style, technique and sound. Just to name a few, musicians like Wes Montgomery, Joe Diorio and Tuck Andres fit into this category. Jimmy Wyble has also developed a unique playing style, technique and sound.

This collection of etudes, written during the decade of the 1970's, were composed as a result of Jimmy's explorations into the musical worlds of counterpoint, harmony and chord melody improvisation for the jazz guitar. The right and left hand fingerings presented in this book were also developed as techniques needed to improvise jazz in two lines. Jimmy uses very standard jazz guitar chord shapes in these etudes, however these shapes move through the harmony in lines rather than block chord structures. This broken chord technique creates a unique contrapuntal sound that separates Jimmy from the rest of the fingerstyle jazz guitar world.

It is hoped that guitarists playing and working through these etudes will see many familiar chord shapes moving in new ways and creating new sounds. These new harmonic sounds combined with beautiful melodies will inspire any guitarist to new levels of musical creativity.

About this edition

When Jimmy first recorded this music, he improvised introductions to many of the etudes. This is the reason for many of the fermatas. Most of the introductions were played out of time. The fermatas solved the problem of trying to accurately notate a rubato improvisation. Jimmy suggests to think of the fermatas as the end of a musical phrase. This lets the music breath and gives it the correct improvisational feel. The music then segues into the original tune usually in swing time. The dotted eighth - sixteenth rhythms in the etudes are written to display swing time. Never play these notes as written. Many of the eighth note passages should also swing although they are not marked. Jimmy also improvised through the changes in some of these passages. When the first edition of the *Art of Two Line Improvisation*, the publisher transcribed Jimmy's improvisations off of the recording. They did a great job, but many small mistakes (mostly engraving errors) were also published. These errors consisted of missing ties, missing accidentals, enharmonic misspellings, eighth note beams missing, wrong notes and missing measures. Many of the etudes had (no or very sparse) left hand fingerings. Jimmy's right and left hand fingerings are crucial to learning this music and to develop a clear understanding of his style and technique. This new edition of the *Art of Two Line Improvisation* has attempted to correct the engraving errors of the first edition as well as adding more right and left hand fingerings and a recording. Tablature has also been added to make the book accessible to the non reading finger style guitarist. Jimmy recommends that if you read tablature that you look often into the music notation for help with the right and left hand fingering.

Examples

The infinite possibilities of our basic source, the scale, are indeed astounding. As growing guitarists there are two areas which we must deal with constantly: the area of efficiency (technique) and the forever expanding area of harmonic awareness (new sounds). We must investigate, research, experiment, and constantly seek new ways.

This section of the book is intended as a brief introduction to the two-line approach. In dealing with the concept of two scales played at the same time great demands are placed on both the right and left hands. It is therefore doubly important that the examples be executed at tempos well within the player's ability. All examples are written in the key of C (unless otherwise indicated); it is imperative that they be transposed into all twelve keys.

It is recommended that all single lines be executed by alternating the right hand thumb and index fingers. While this varies from the traditional classical practice, many players have increased their facility with this technique. The right hand fingerings presented in the examples and in the etudes show passages where this alternation is essential to the correct performance of this music. The right hand fingerings are written on two lines below the music. This should help the guitarist understand the separation of the two different parts in the right hand. These fingerings also make clear the importance of the thumb and index finger alternation and the right hand finger independence needed to play Jimmy Wyble's music.

Example 1 is the scale used throughout these opening examples. This scale is also used in Etudes 17 and 20. The original edition analyzed this scale as a major scale with a lowered third and a raised fourth and fifth. This scale can also be thought of as a modified C diminished scale minus one note, the note "F".

Examples 2 - 7 illustrate the use of the pedal tone as the simplest contrapuntal technique. The player should experiment with placing the pedal tone in the lower voice as well. The second measure varies another parameter by rhythmically displacing the upper voice.

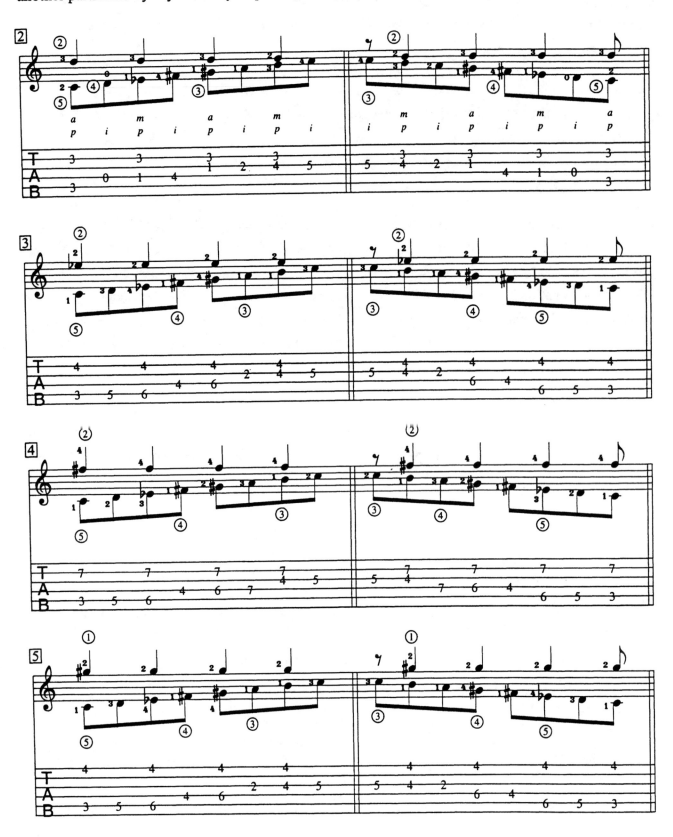

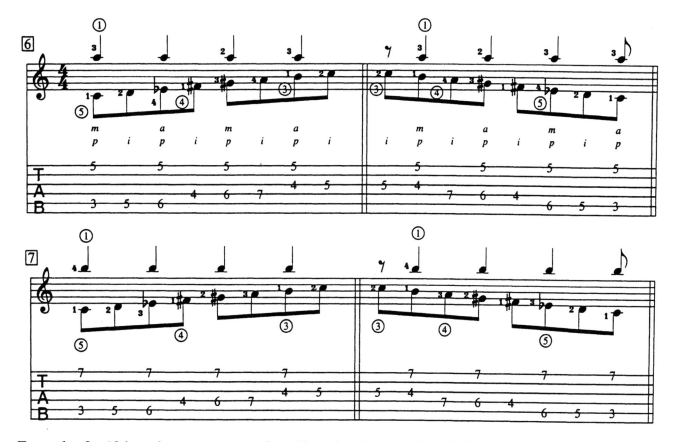

Examples 8 - 13 introduce contrary motion. Note that there is a 2:1-relationship in the number of notes in the lower and the upper voices.

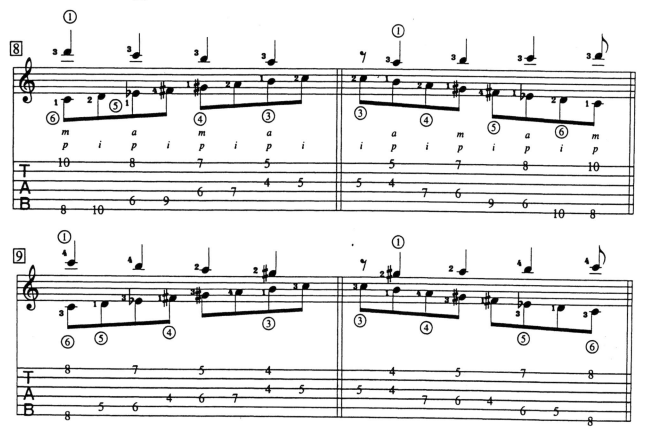

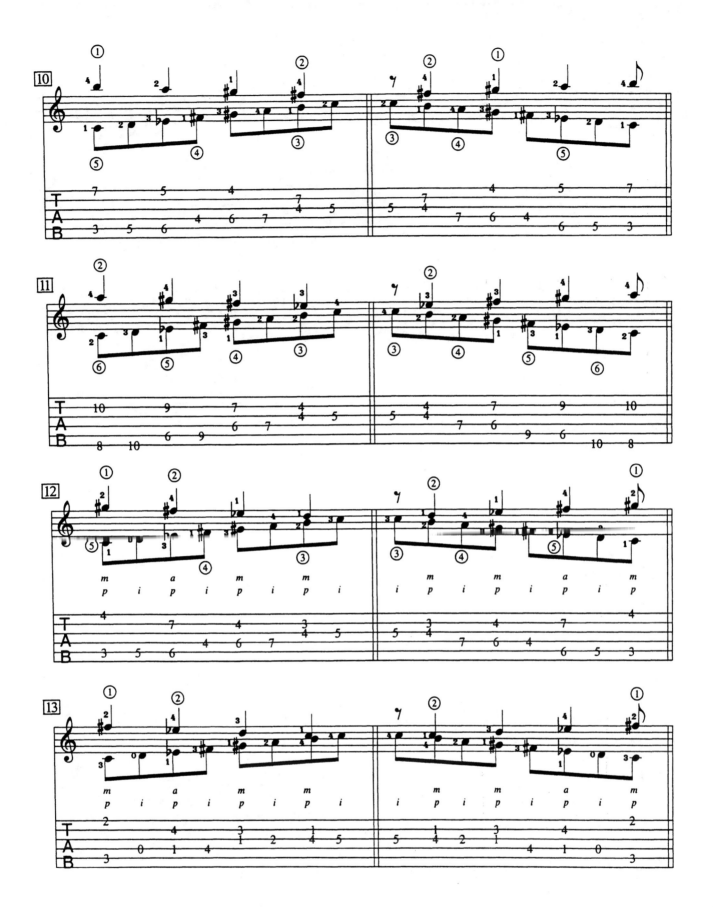

Examples 14 - 17 change the ratio from 2:1 to 1:1

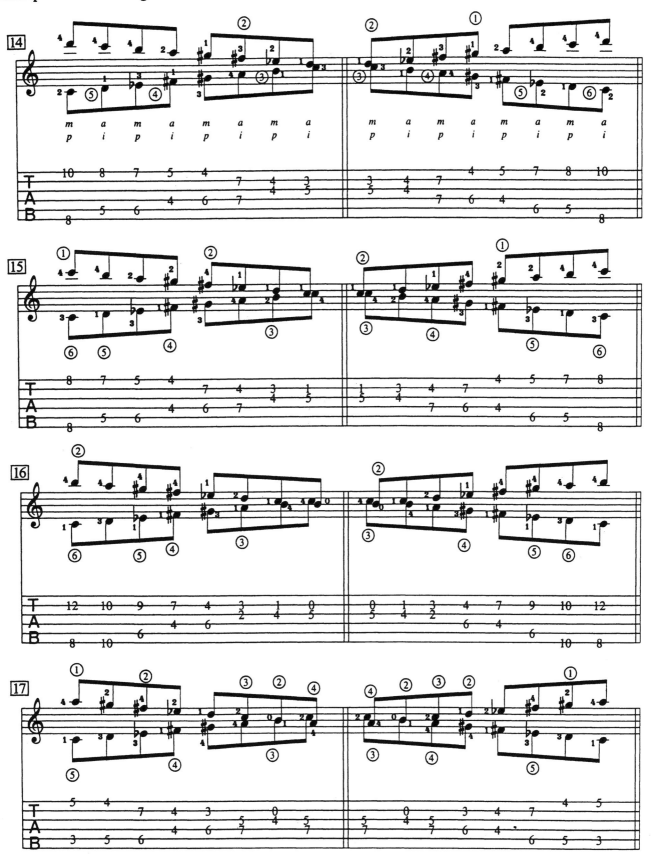

Examples 18 and 19 illustrate syncopation as a result of a 3:1 ratio of notes. Example 19 varies the direction of a voice (the upper) for the first time.

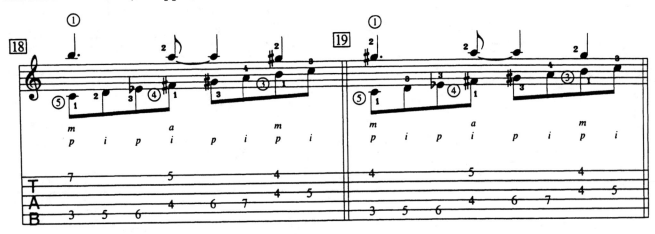

Example 20 and 21 remove the restriction of step-wise movement.

Example 22 introduces two new concepts: chromatic tones and octave displacement. Notice that the note names of the lower voice (E♭, D, D♭, C) describe a chromatic line, yet raising the D♭ one octave produces fresh sound.

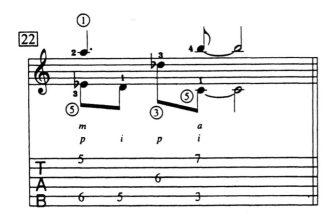

Example 23 takes Example 22 through the circle of fifths.

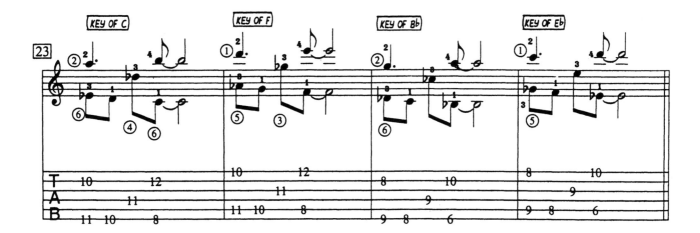

ETUDE SEVEN

JIMMY WYBLE

HOLD FERMATA ONLY ON FINE

FINE

9

ETUDE EIGHT

Jimmy Wyble

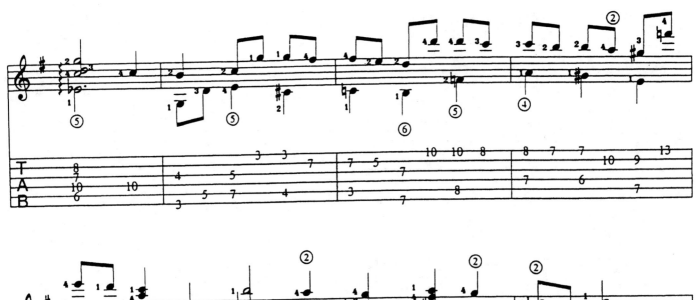

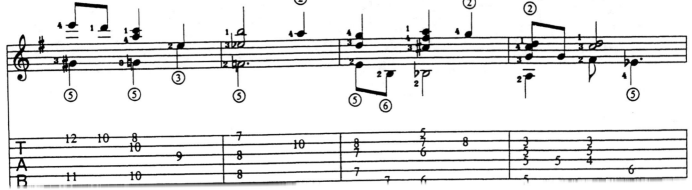

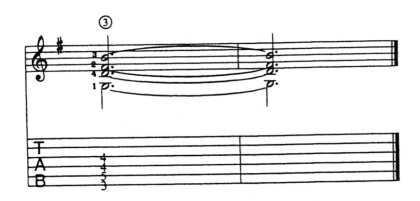

ETUDE NINE

JIMMY WYBLE

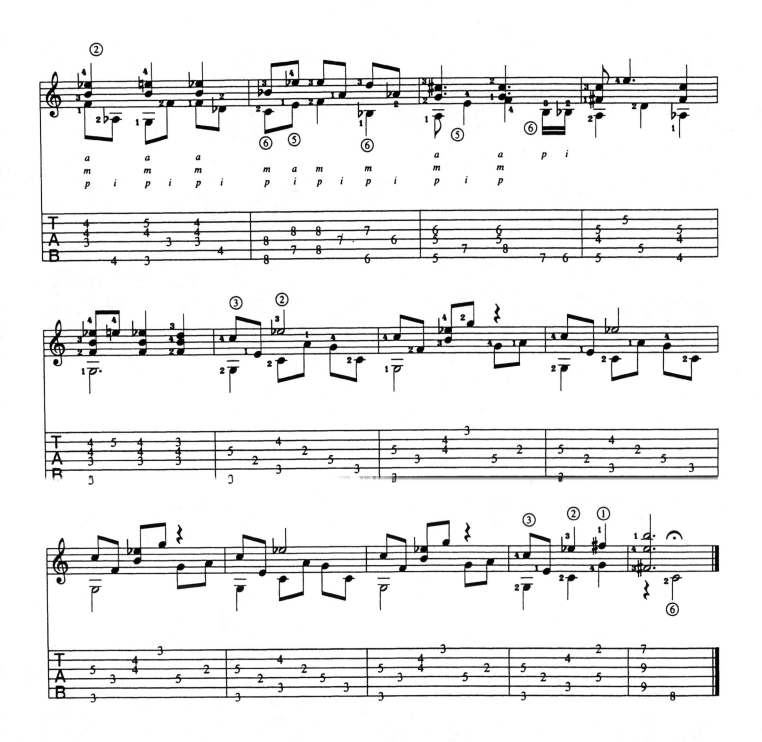

ETUDE TEN

(to Scott Joplin)

JIMMY WYBLE

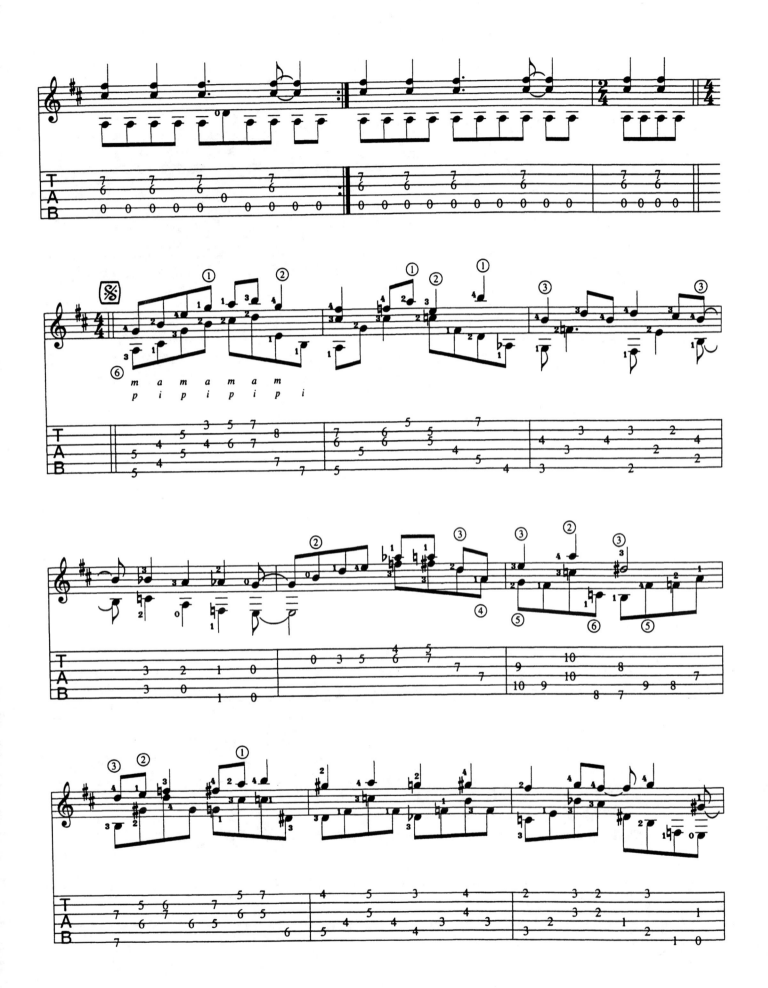

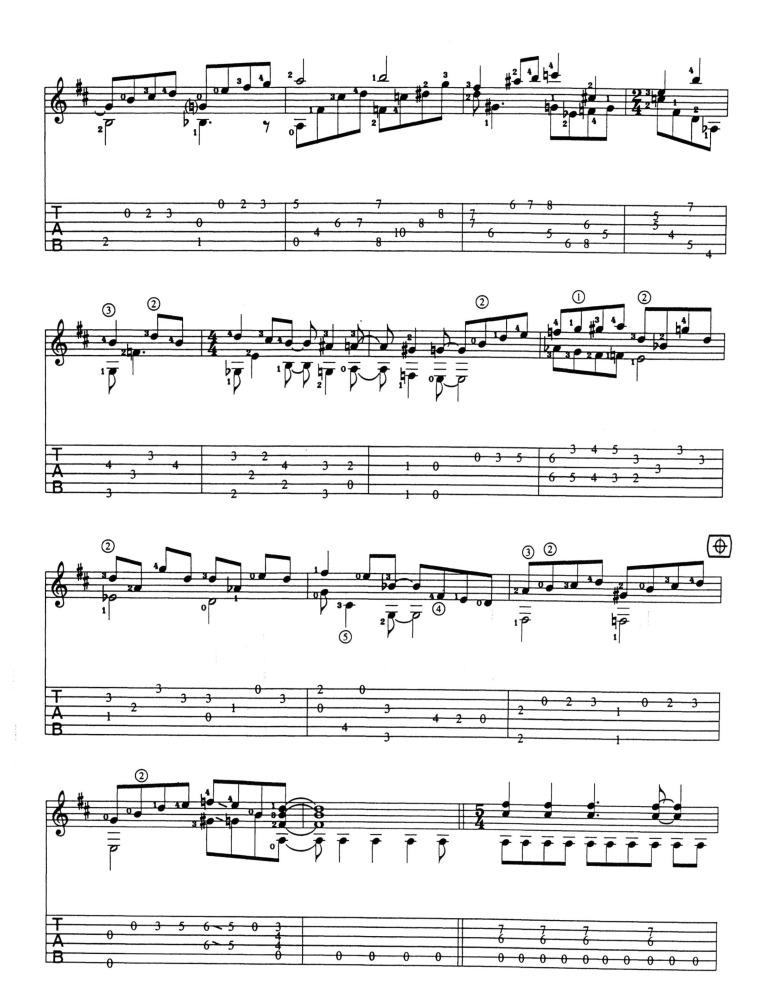

27

ETUDE ELEVEN

(Blues for Bix)

JIMMY WYBLE

ETUDE TWELVE

(to Red Norvo)

JIMMY WYBLE

ETUDE THIRTEEN

(to Jimmy Rowles)

JIMMY WYBLE

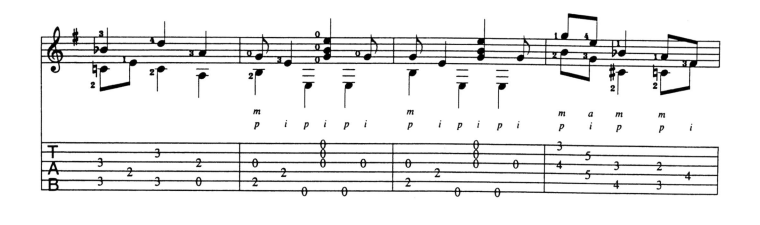

43

ETUDE FOURTEEN

to Alec Wilder

JIMMY WYBLE

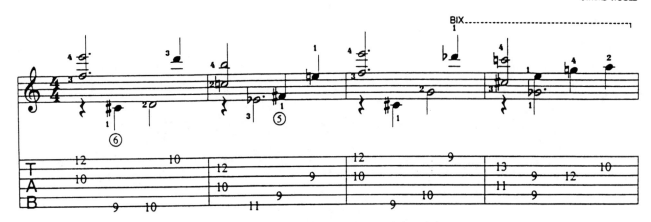

ETUDE FIFTEEN

to Alec Wilder

JIMMY WYBLE

This page has been left blank to avoid awkward page turns

ETUDE SIXTEEN

to Alec Wilder

Jimmy Wyble

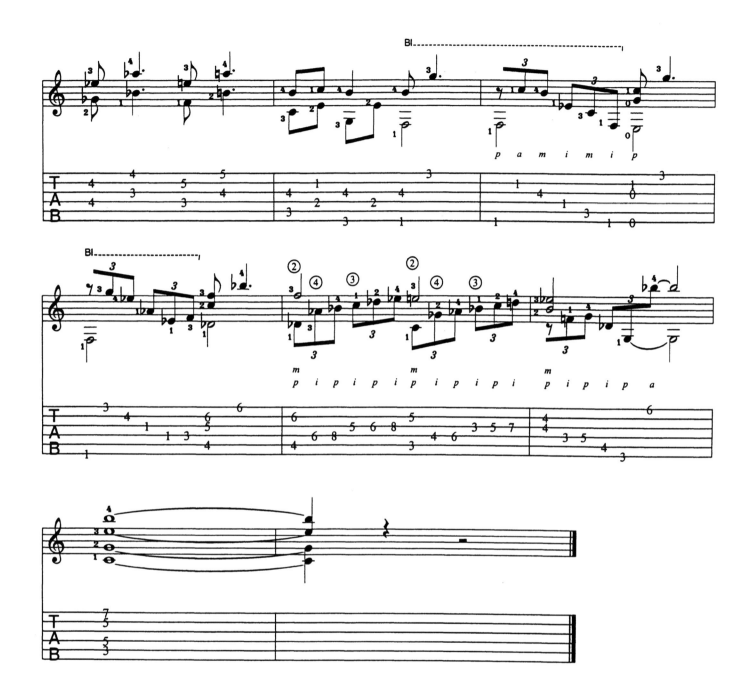

ETUDE SEVENTEEN

(to Fats Waller)

JIMMY WYBLE

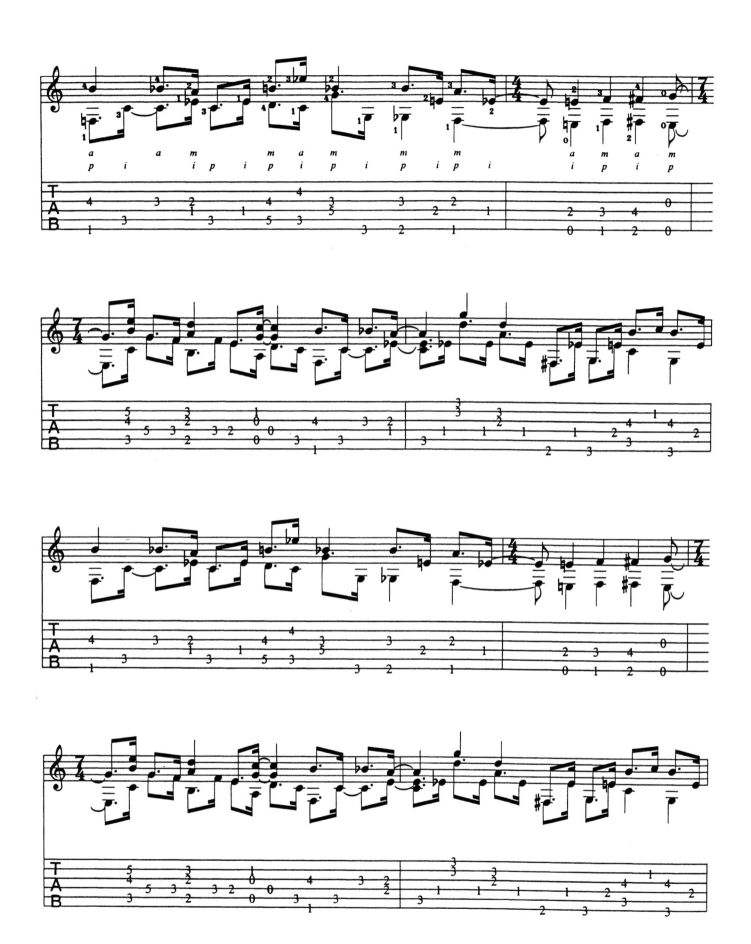

51

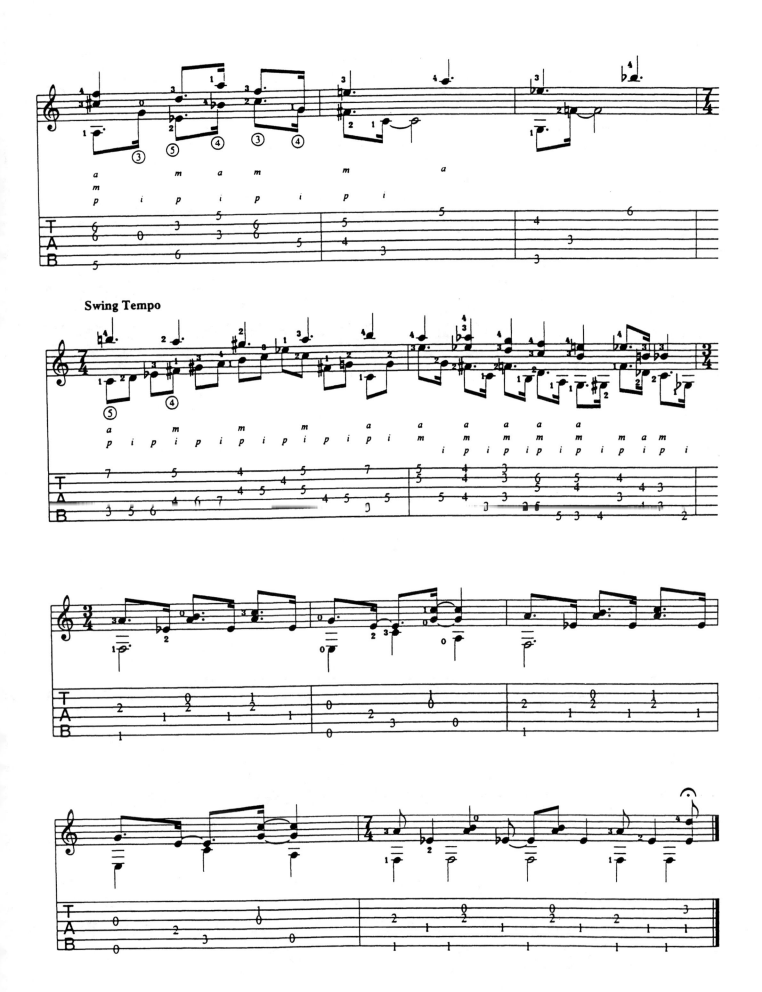

This page has been left blank to avoid awkward page turns

ETUDE EIGHTEEN

JIMMY WYBLE

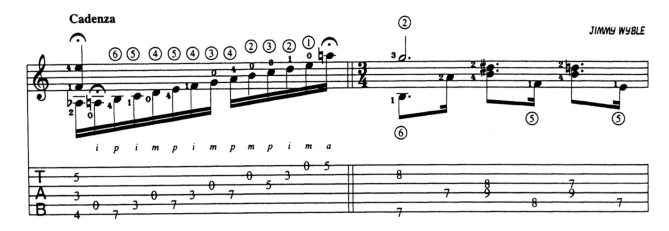

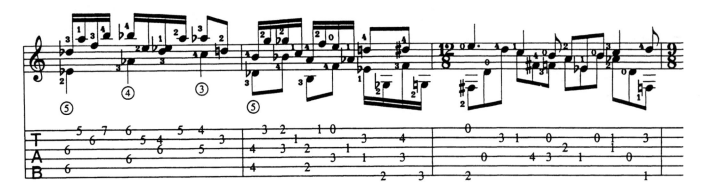

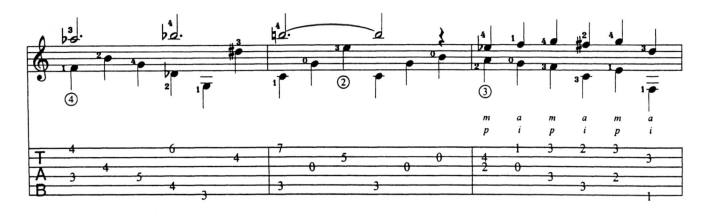

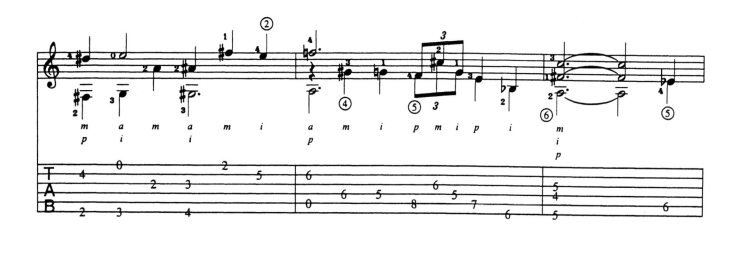

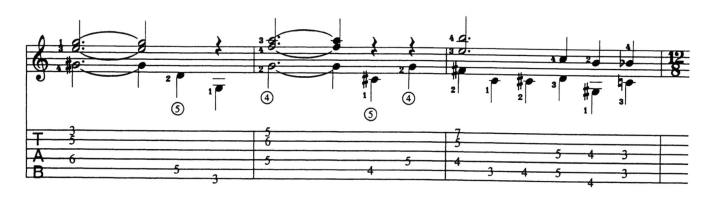

ETUDE NINETEEN

(Blues for Monk)

JIMMY WYBLE

59

ETUDE TWENTY

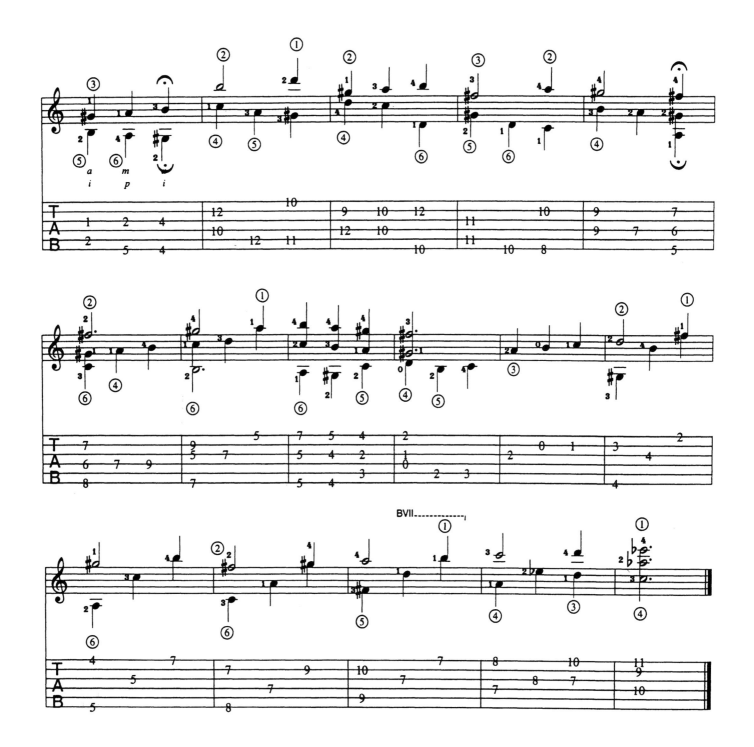

ETUDE TWENTY-ONE

(Two Lines for Barney)

JIMMY WYBLE

ETUDE TWENTY-TWO

(to Louis Armstrong)

JIMMY WYBLE

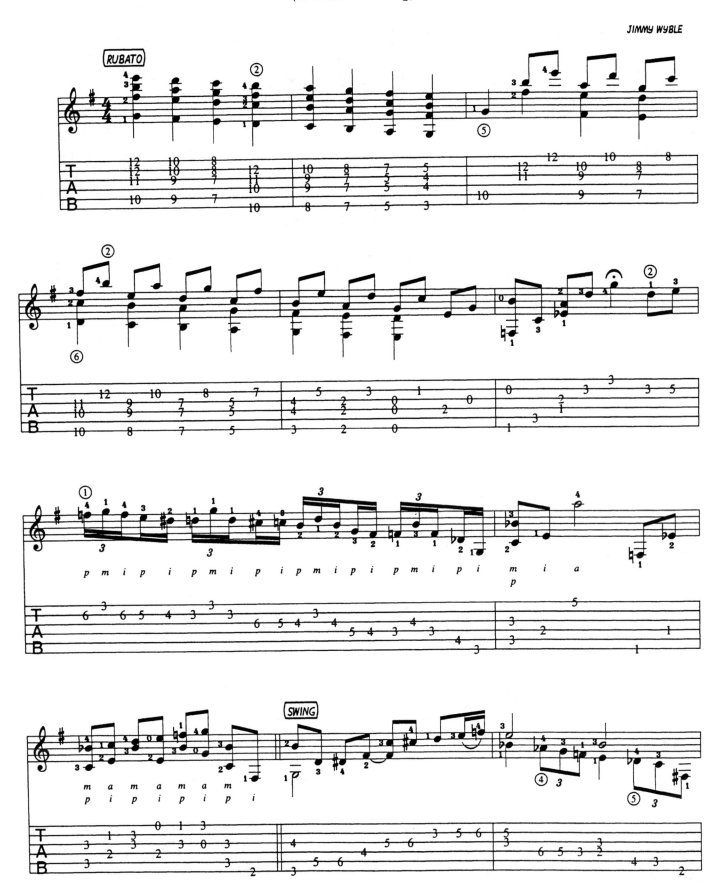

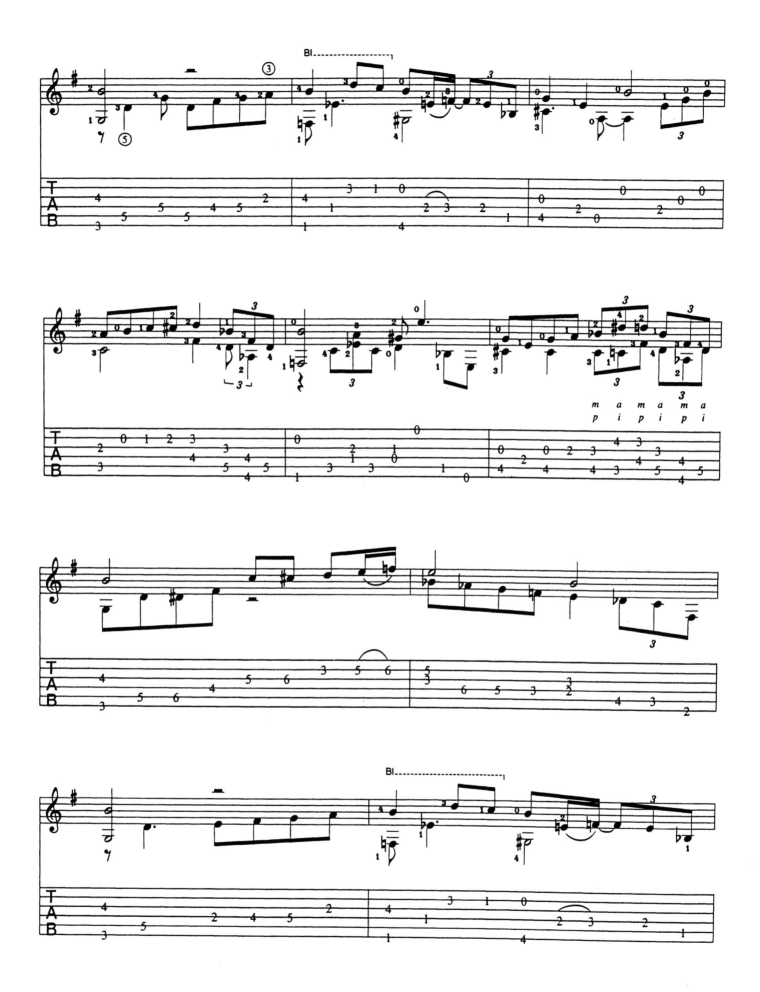

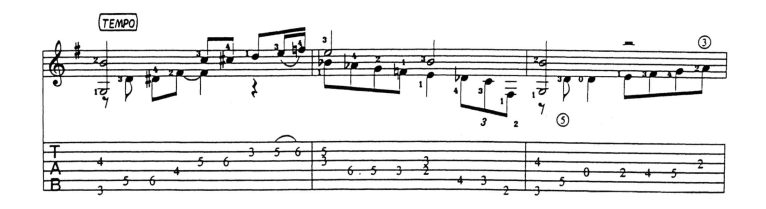

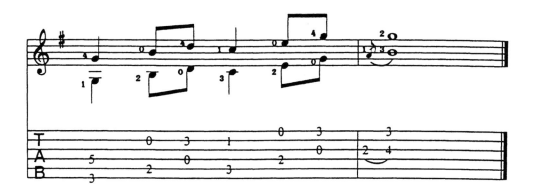

ETUDE TWENTY-THREE

(Jigsaw)

JIMMY WYBLE

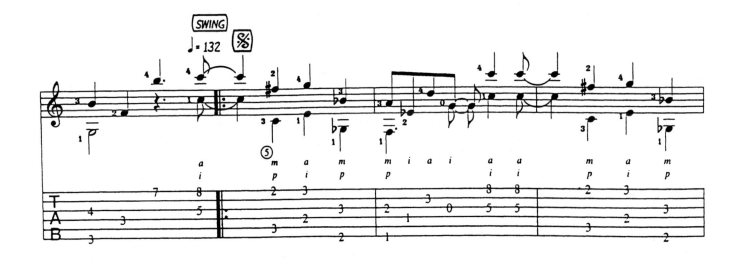

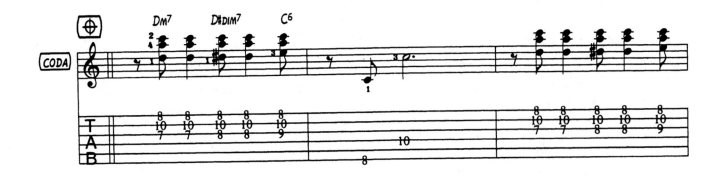

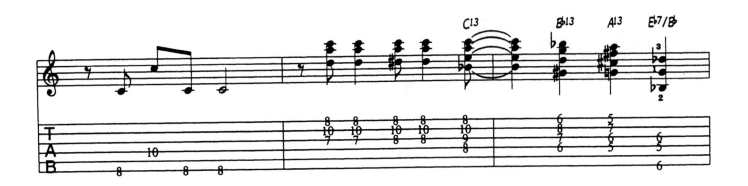

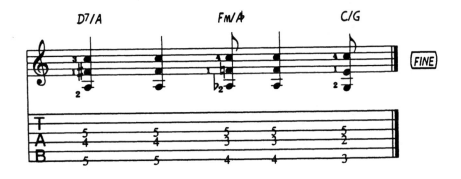

Performance note:
Play the C octaves only at the repeat sign when repeating. (Follow the tie directions) Do not play the octaves when going on to the bridge or the coda. Treat the eighth note A natural on beat four of that measure as a full quarter note.

*This page has been
left blank to avoid
awkward page turns*

ETUDE TWENTY-FOUR
(The Silent One)

JIMMY WYBLE

ETUDE TWENTY-FIVE

JIMMY WYBLE

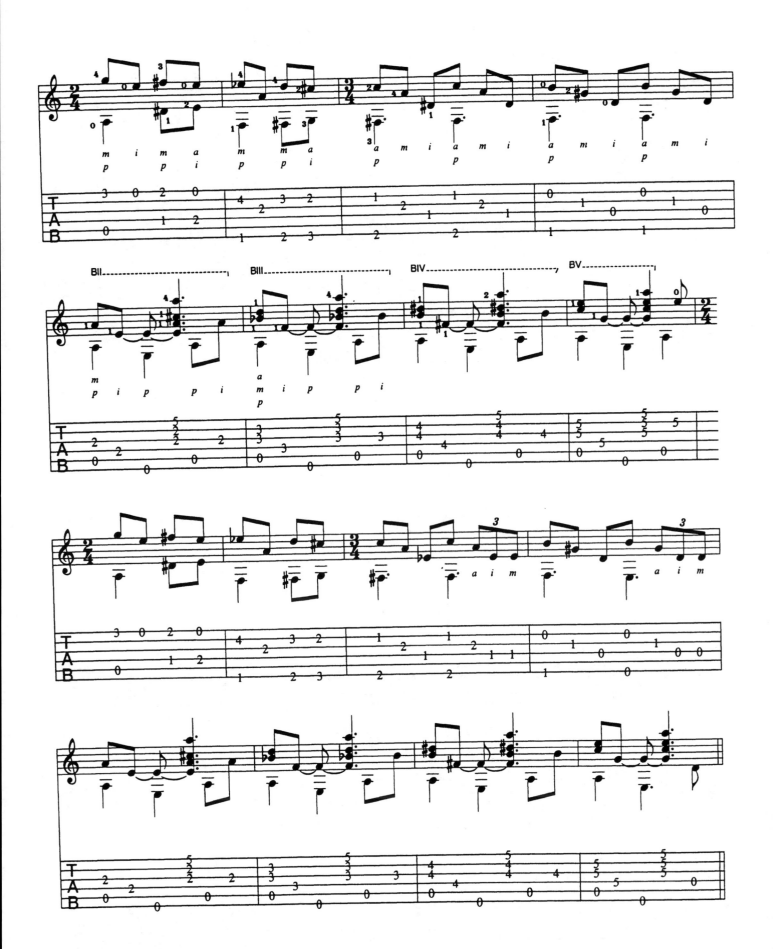

80

IMPROVISATION PART ONE

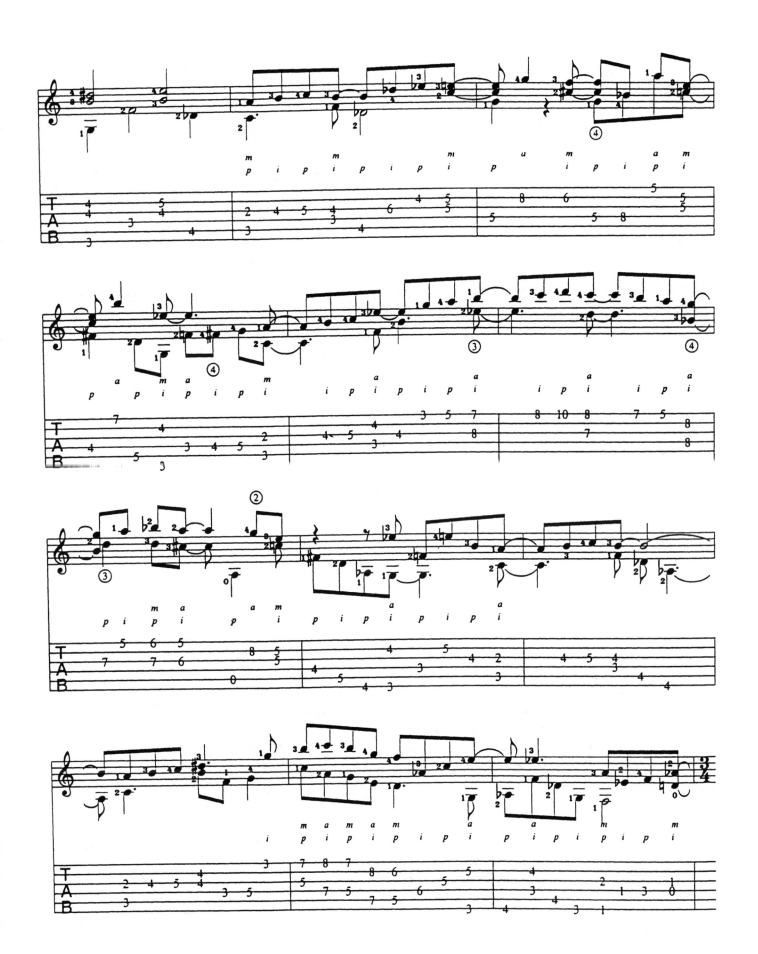

84

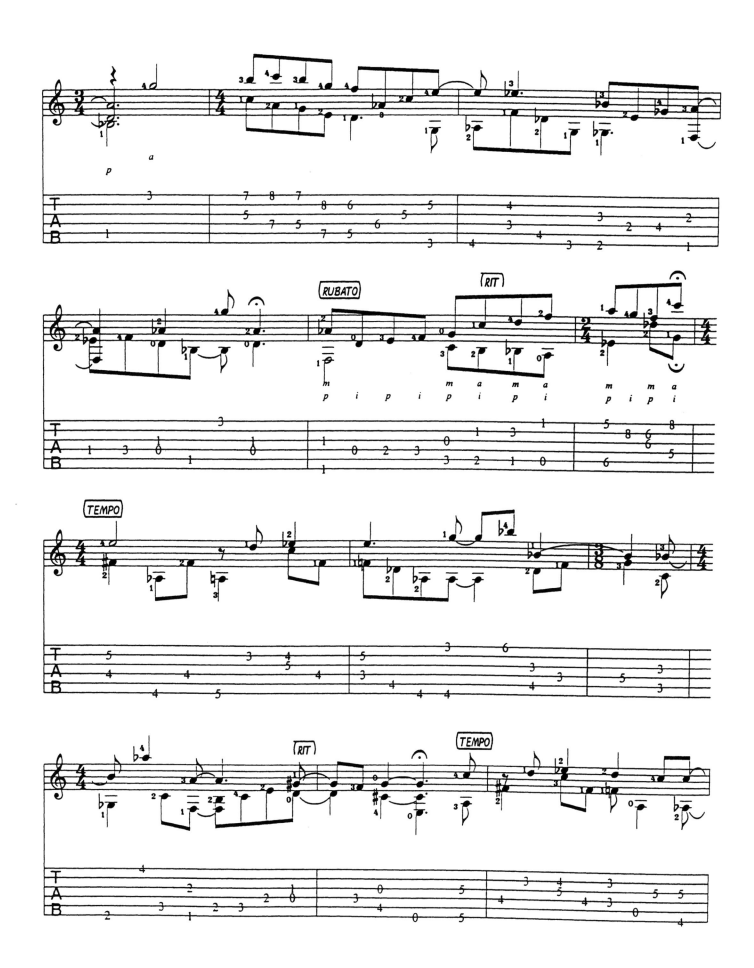

IMPROVISATION PART TWO

JIMMY WYBLE